I'M GLAD THERE ARE...

Trees and Other Plants

By Tracey Turner

Illustrated by Fiona Powers

WINDMILL BOOKS

Published in 2025 by Windmill Books,
an Imprint of Rosen Publishing
2544 Clinton St.
Buffalo, NY 14224

First published in Great Britain in 2022 by The Watts Publishing Group

Credits
Design and project management: Raspberry Books
Art Direction and cover design: Sidonie Beresford-Browne
Design: Kathryn Davies
Illustration: Fiona Powers

Cataloging-in-Publication Data

Names: Turner, Tracey, author. | Powers, Fiona, illustrator.
Title: Trees and other plants / by Tracey Turner, illustrated by Fiona Powers.
Description: Buffalo, New York : Windmill Books, 2025. | Series: I'm glad there are... | Includes glossary and index.
Identifiers: ISBN 9781538396438 (pbk.) | ISBN 9781538396445 (library bound) | ISBN 9781538396452 (ebook)
Subjects: LCSH: Trees--Juvenile literature. | Plants--Juvenile literature.
Classification: LCC QK475.8 T87 2025 | DDC 582.16--dc23

Printed in the United States of America
CPSIA Compliance Information: Batch #CSWM25: For Further Information contact Rosen Publishing at 1-800-237-9932

I'M GLAD THERE ARE...

Trees and Other Plants

By **Tracey Turner**

Illustrated by **Fiona Powers**

WINDMILL BOOKS

Contents

I'M GLAD THERE ARE

Trees and Other Plants

I LOVE PLANTS! They are homes for all sorts of animals, like monkeys, squirrels, and birds, and provide them with things to eat.

They give us delicious food, from strawberries and potatoes to bread and rice.

They can be beautiful, like this lovely passionflower.

We can use them as medicines.

They help planet Earth breathe. They are all amazing!

ONE-THIRD of planet EARTH is covered in trees. There are tens of thousands of different kinds.

You don't have to look very far to find a tree or a plant, even if you live in the middle of a city. Just go outside and look around!

I'M GLAD THERE ARE

Trees

...because they keep planet Earth alive.

TREES are beautiful to look at, and they're also really important. We couldn't live without them!

Instead of eating, trees absorb carbon dioxide (the same gas we breathe out) and use sunlight to turn the carbon dioxide and rainwater into food. They produce oxygen (which is in the air) as part of the process.

ALL animals need oxygen to breathe.

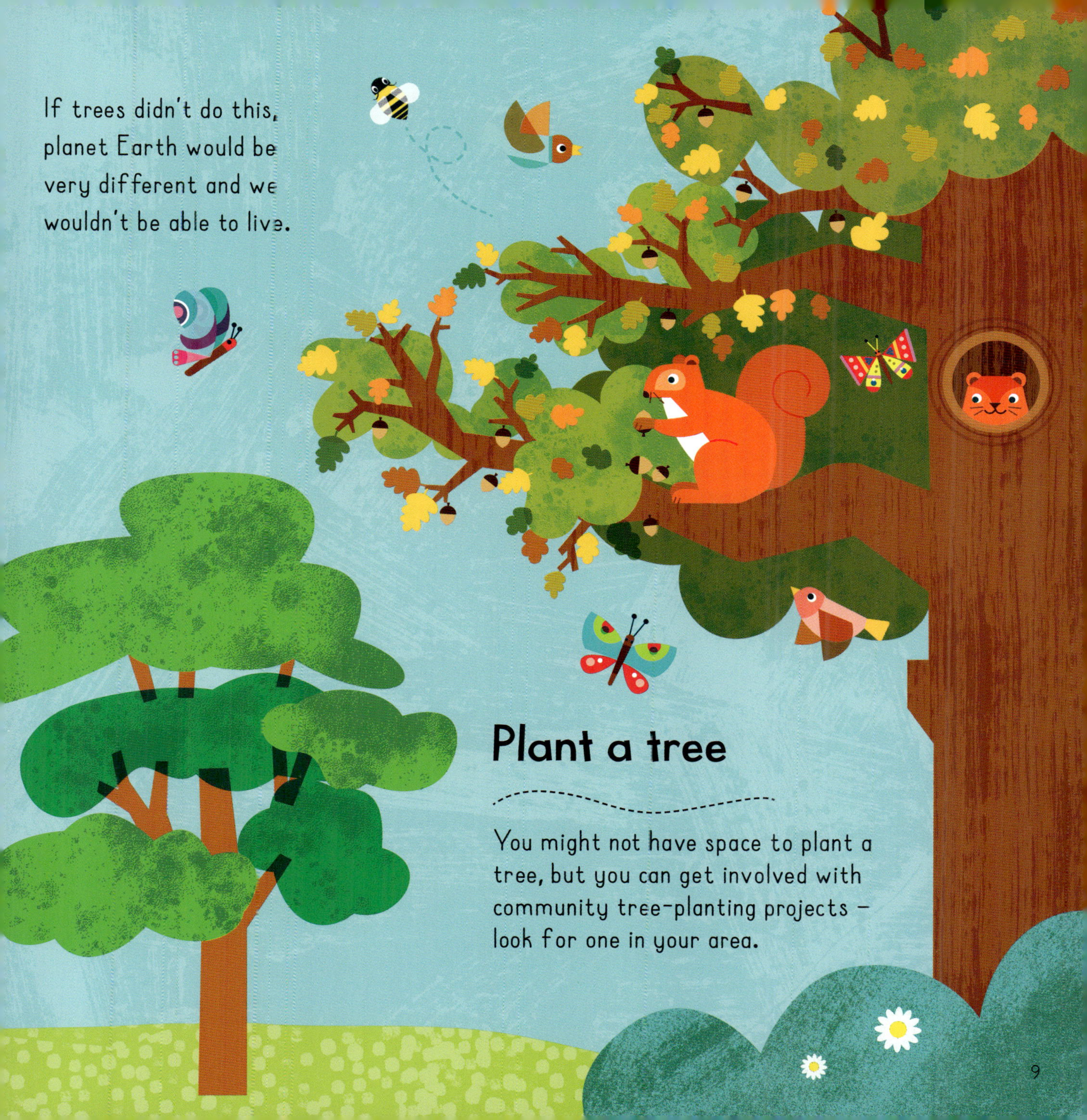

If trees didn't do this, planet Earth would be very different and we wouldn't be able to live.

Plant a tree

You might not have space to plant a tree, but you can get involved with community tree-planting projects – look for one in your area.

I'M GLAD THERE ARE

Trees for Birds

...because they are home many of Earth's birds.

Most BIRDS rely on trees because they build their nests in them. Bald eagles build their nests in really big trees because their nests are HUGE – the length of a car!

I love listening to birds singing. In spring or summer, I sometimes get up just as it starts to get light, then open a window and listen as the birds start to wake up and call to one another. It's an amazing sound, known as the dawn chorus.

Birds make other sounds, too. Woodpeckers peck tree trunks to make their nests and to reach bugs inside the wood. Instead of singing, they drum against trees to tell one another where they are.

I'M GLAD THERE ARE

Deciduous Trees

...because they're a sign of the changing seasons!

The first green buds on trees are a sign that SPRING has arrived and there's warmer weather to come. You might hear baby birds chirping in their nests.

In SUMMER, deciduous trees are green and full of life. The baby birds grow up and learn to fly.

In **AUTUMN**, the leaves of deciduous trees start to change color, die, and drop off. Crunching through piles of autumn leaves is fun!

In **WINTER**, deciduous trees have bare branches. But they can still be beautiful.

Climb a tree

Climbing trees is one of my favorite things! Before you climb, ask a grown-up to help find a tree that's safe, and to be there to help in case you get stuck.

I'M GLAD THERE ARE

Evergreens

...because they add color to cold winter days.

EVERGREENS are plants that don't shed all their leaves, so they are green all year round. In a cold, gray winter, the world would look very dull without them!

Most evergreen trees are conifers, which have hard, sometimes spiky leaves. They include the world's tallest trees. A coast redwood in California measures 380 feet (116 m) tall – the tallest tree alive today.

The heaviest thing in the world is a conifer, too! Giant sequoias grow in California and can weigh more than 6,000 tons (5,500 tonnes).

Grow an evergreen

Not all evergreens are big. You could grow heather in a pot or a window box. They have flowers, and different kinds flower at different times of the year.

Flowers

...because they look and smell lovely.

My favorite PLANTS are ones that have flowers – lilies, roses, and jasmine all look beautiful and smell wonderful. There are hundreds of thousands of different kinds of flowers.

The colors and smells of flowers tell insects that there's sweet nectar for them to drink. They suck up the nectar, and at the same time they move pollen from one flower to another, which helps make seeds to grow new plants.

I love watching the bees, butterflies, and other insects as they buzz from bloom to bloom.

Plant flower seeds

Ask an adult to help you plant some seeds that will turn into colorful flowers. Nasturtium seeds are easy to grow – plant them in spring for bright orange blooms in summer.

I'M GLAD THERE ARE

Plants We Can Eat

...because they're delicious!

We eat different parts of PLANTS – fruit, seeds, leaves, and roots . . .

All fruit begins with a flower. Strawberries, oranges, blueberries, and apples were all flowers before they turned into tasty fruit. Pumpkins, zucchini, and cucumbers start off as flowers, too.

We eat the roots or tubers of some plants, including potatoes, carrots, and beetroot, and the green leaves of others, like cabbages and lettuce.

We use the seeds, or grains, of other plants for food. Rice is a seed, and we grind wheat seeds to make bread.

Grow potatoes

In springtime, find an old potato that's starting to send out little sprouts. Plant it in the ground or in a pot and it should grow into a leafy plant. A few months later, it's time to dig it up – you should find potatoes among the roots!

I'M GLAD THERE ARE

Desert Plants

...because they're fascinating water storers.

Even where there's hardly any water, plants can thrive! DESERT PLANTS have clever ways of finding and storing water.

Some desert plants have really long roots – the length of two buses! – to find water deep underground.

Cactus plants collect rainwater with their roots, then store it in their flesh. They can live for years without rain. Instead of leaves they have sharp spines, which protect them from animals. Cacti are flowering plants, and produce beautiful, colorful blooms.

Resurrection plants are desert plants that dry up completely when there's no water. They look brown and dead, and blow around the desert like tumbleweed. But they're not dead at all – when it rains, or the plants find water, they drink and open up green, ferny fronds.

I'M GLAD THERE ARE

Grasslands

...because they're home to some of the most amazing animals on Earth.

GRASSES take over where there isn't enough rain for many trees to live. They keep growing even when animals nibble on them, so big herds of grazing animals can happily chomp away.

Grasslands are called different things around the world. In Africa they're called savannas and veldts, in North America they're prairies, in Asia they're known as steppes, and in South America they're called pampas and cerrados.

The African savanna is home to a wide variety of animals. Zebras, wildebeest, and antelope are some of the animals that eat the grass. Lions, cheetahs, and leopards prey on the grazing animals.

I'M GLAD THERE ARE

Forests

...because some of my favorite animals live there.

BIG ANIMALS like bears, wolves, and moose live in the wild forests of Alaska in the United States, eating the plants and animals they find there.

In the forests of northern Europe, you might see squirrels, or a red fox or a badger at dawn or dusk. Small animals like mice make their homes there, too, along with thousands of different kinds of insects.

A Walk in the Woods

Go for a walk in the forest with a trusted grown-up. Find somewhere to sit, then don't move or speak for as long as you can. How many animals can you see and hear?

My favorite animal of all is the panda. It lives in the forests of China, where it eats bamboo leaves.

I'M GLAD THERE ARE

Rainforests

...because they are bursting with life.

The AMAZON is the biggest rainforest in the world. It's full of tens of thousands of different kinds of plants, including the walking palm tree, which has roots like stilts! Amazon plants have been used to make medicines.

The plants of the Amazon shelter millions of animals, including colorful birds like parrots and toucans.

There are 2.5 million different types of insects, and thousands of kinds of fish, birds, reptiles, and other animals in the Amazon rainforest. It's also home to the world's biggest beetle (the titan beetle) and the world's smallest monkey (the pygmy marmoset).

Rainforests get their name because they get a LOT of rainfall – up to 10 feet (3 m) every year!

I'M GLAD THERE ARE

Houseplants

...because they bring nature inside.

HOUSEPLANTS are great because everyone can grow them! An easy one to grow is Monstera, also known as a Swiss cheese plant.

Plants that grow where it's warm all year round and don't need too much light can make good indoor plants. Lots of houseplants are originally from tropical parts of the world, where they grow on the forest floor.

Growing plants indoors

Most plants need quite a lot of natural light, so put them close to a window. Don't water them too much – overwatering is most likely to kill a houseplant! Make sure the pots have drainage holes.

GLOSSARY

Absorb
to soak up, like a sponge soaks up water.

Cactus
a plant with a thick, fleshy stem, spines instead of leaves, and brightly colored flowers.

Carbon dioxide
a gas (though it can also become solid if it's very cold). People and animals breathe out carbon dioxide.

Deciduous plants
plants that shed all of their leaves in winter.

Evergreen plants
plants that don't shed all of their leaves at the same time.

Frond
a leaf, or a leaflike part of a plant.

Graze
to feed on grass.

Insect
a small animal with six legs, three parts to its body, and a hard outer shell called an exoskeleton.

Nectar
a sweet liquid made inside flowers.

Oxygen
a gas that's part of the air we breathe. All animals need oxygen to live.

Rainforest
a forest that has more than 8 feet (2.5 m) of rainfall every year. As well as tropical rainforests, such as the Amazon, there are rainforests in temperate parts of the world.

Roots
the part of a plant that attaches it to the ground and carries water and food to the rest of the plant. Roots are usually, but not always, underground.

Savanna
grassy plains with few trees.

Temperate regions
parts of the world with seasonal changes and generally mild climates.

Tree
a woody plant, usually with a single trunk bearing branches.

Tropical
describes warm regions close to the equator, the imaginary line that goes around the middle of Earth.

Tuber
an underground part of a plant stem, from which new plants can grow.

INDEX